Kip

A SEA OTTER

by Bonnie Highsmith Taylor

Perfection Learning®

Cover Photo: Jeff Foott (www.jfoot.com)

Dedication
For Friends of the Sea Otter

About the Author
Bonnie Highsmith Taylor is a native Oregonian. She loves camping in the Oregon mountains and watching birds and other wildlife. Writing is Ms. Taylor's first love. But she also enjoys going to plays and concerts, collecting antique dolls, and listening to good music.

Image Credits

Jeff Foott (www.jfoot.com) pp. 5, 7, 8, 11–24, 25, 30–42, 47, 48, 50, 52–54. Corel Professional Photos pp. 6, 9, 10, 26, 28, 29, 38, 43–45, 49, 51.

CONTENTS

CHAPTER 1

It was late at night. There was no moon or stars.

It was quiet. Ocean waves made the only sounds as they lapped against large rocks.

Not far from the beach were kelp beds. Groups of sea otters slept in the kelp.

These groups are called *rafts*. The adult males usually stay in one raft. The females and the pups stay in another.

The sea otters slept on their backs. Each had strands of kelp wrapped around its body. The kelp kept the otters from floating away.

There were about 20 females and pups in one raft. One of the females stirred. She was very restless. She was due to have her first pup.

She pushed away the strands of seaweed. She rolled over and over in the water. She felt sharp little pains in her lower belly.

It was time. She made her way to the shore.

She had mated a little over eight months ago. That was in late July. Most animals have a certain time for breeding. But sea otters mate any time of the year.

The female otter found a flat rock on the shore. She climbed on it and lay on her back. She raised her upper body. Then she lowered it. She seemed to be doing sit-ups. She strained, making low grunting sounds.

In a short time, her pup was born. Unlike many mammals, Kip was born with his eyes open. Kittens' and puppies' eyes don't open until they are nearly two

weeks old. A bear cub's eyes don't open until it is six weeks old.

Kip was also born with teeth. And he had a thick coat of fur. He was a little over 16 inches long. He weighed three pounds. The female's future pups would weigh more—about four pounds.

The mother otter cleaned her pup for over an hour. She used her tongue and paws.

She lifted him up. Then she turned him to face her nipples. A female otter has only two nipples. They are on her lower belly.

Sea otters have just one pup at a time. They are born about every other year. There have been a few cases of twin pups being born. But usually one or both died at birth.

It would be hard for a mother otter to raise two pups at once. First, she carries the pup almost everywhere the first year. Second, she would not have enough milk.

Kip nursed noisily. His mother continued to clean him. She fluffed his fur. She nuzzled him with her nose.

Kip filled his stomach with warm, sweet milk. Then he slept.

The female otter grew nervous. She had been away from the kelp bed for a long time. Sea otters do not spend much time out of the water.

Danger would come with daylight. An eagle could carry her baby away.

She tucked Kip under one arm. Then she swam back to the kelp bed. She lay on her back.

Once more she wrapped a strand of seaweed around her body. She cuddled Kip close to her. He made soft sniffling sounds as he slept.

CHAPTER 2

The next morning, several young otters came close. They wanted to see the new pup. They sniffed him all over.

One young otter licked some milk from the pup's mouth. Kip nuzzled the young otter. He made a cooing sound. He was so happy.

Kip's mother watched closely. But she was not upset. She was curious. Otters are very curious. And they are playful and loving.

The mother otter was hungry. She had not eaten for a while. The last time had been several hours before Kip was born.

Sea otters have huge appetites. They eat as much as a fifth of their body weight every day—about 3,000 calories. They eat abalones, clams, crabs, and mussels. They also eat octopuses, sea urchins, squid, and snails. Sometimes they find impets, sea cucumbers, and fish.

Sea otters do not catch a lot of fish. They are not very fast swimmers. When they do catch fish, they don't eat them whole. Most other sea animals do.

Instead, otters tear the fish into chunks. And they chew their food well before swallowing.

Otters eat a lot of sea urchins. This is helpful. If sea urchins are not kept under control, they destroy the kelp. And many ocean animals depend on the kelp beds.

Otters often eat so many sea urchins that their teeth and bones turn purple. This is caused by a chemical in the urchins.

The mother otter set Kip on a bed of kelp. She wrapped a strand of the kelp around his body. Then she dived down into the water.

Sea otters can dive over 180 feet if they need to. They can hold their breath for five minutes.

This time the female otter was in a hurry. She did not want to leave her pup alone for long.

She surfaced quickly. She held a clam in one mittenlike paw. She carried something else in her other paw. It was a flat rock shaped like a plate.

She lifted her baby from his kelp cradle. Then she turned on her back. Her baby nursed on her lower body.

The female put the flat rock on her chest. She banged the clam against it. Finally, it broke open. Then she sucked out the good, juicy meat.

Kip let go of the nipple. He made his way to where his mother was eating. He sniffed at the clam meat.

Kip did not care for the smell. It would be a long time before Kip would eat solid food. For now, all he wanted was his mother's milk.

Kip filled his stomach until it would hold no more. He was tired. Nursing was hard work. He wanted a nap.

The female otter was sleepy too. But first, she needed a bath. Her fur was covered with bits of shell and clam juice.

Once more, she placed her pup on a kelp bed. Over and over, she rolled in the water. She turned again on her back. She squeezed the water from her thick fur with her paws.

She set Kip on her chest. She cleaned him for a long time. She licked him. And she blew into his fur to fluff it.

Kip's mother was still hungry. But she did not like leaving him alone while she searched for food. For the first few days, she fed mostly at night. There was less danger from eagles and other enemies.

Mother sea otters are very protective of their young. They guard them closely. And they spend a lot of time playing with their pups and teaching them.

Kip fell asleep on his mother's

stomach. The female also slept. She covered her eyes with her paws to keep out the bright sunlight. She made soft cooing sounds in her sleep.

Other otters floated on their backs around Kip and his mother. Other females also had young pups.

Many of the older pups played together. They played tag. They made chuckling noises as they romped in the water.

Sometimes their play got too rough. A loud cry would bring a mother to her pup's rescue.

Adult otters also play. They play with their pups and with other otters. They will bat a piece of seaweed around. They toss it into the air and swat it before it hits the water.

Sea otters love to turn somersaults under the water. Few animals are more playful than sea otters. That is why they are called "sea clowns" and "clowns of the kelp beds."

CHAPTER 3

No baby ever received more love and care than Kip. Not even a human baby.

Kip's mother floated on her back. She cuddled her baby in her arms. She blew on his fur. And she nuzzled him with her nose. She made cooing noises. It was as if she were singing him a lullaby.

There is a close bond between a mother and her pup. Even when the mother has her next pup, the older one may stay with her. She spends a whole year or more caring for her pup. She teaches it to dive and hunt for food.

Diving is difficult to learn. Otters float easily because their fur is so thick.

Pups have to learn how to push themselves downward. They use an up-and-down motion with their webbed hind feet and their tails.

Kip's mother taught him how to roll over and over in the water to clean himself. And she taught him how to avoid danger.

Kip's mother tucked him into a seaweed cradle. She wrapped him in kelp leaves. He would be safe here.

Then she dived deep in the water. She looked for food. She was tired of sea urchins. She wanted something different.

Karl Kenyon, a man who studied sea otters, told of seeing a female otter carrying a dead pup. She had brought it out of the water. She laid it on the kelp-covered rocks. For nearly an hour, she cleaned it. When it was dry, she nestled it on her chest and went to sleep.

At last, she found it. A big abalone was stuck tightly to a rock. It was nearly ten inches long. The otter tugged at it. But she could not pull it loose.

After about three minutes, she had to go up for air. Then down she went again. This time she found a heavy rock. She pounded at the abalone until it broke loose.

Up she came. She carried a choice meal. She took her baby from his cradle. She turned him around on her body. He latched hungrily onto a nipple.

While her pup nursed, Kip's mother enjoyed the juicy white meat of the abalone.

She washed away the bits of shell and juice. Now it was time for a nap. She lay on her back and closed her eyes. She and her pup slept.

Suddenly, the female woke with a start. Something was wrong. She threw up her arms in alarm. She hurriedly placed Kip in a kelp bed.

She stood upright in the water. She shaded her eyes with her paws. But all she could see were high waves. The wind began to howl.

She grabbed Kip and tucked him under her arm. She swam for the shore. Other otters were racing for the shore too. Mothers carried their pups.

She could swim up to ten miles per hour. But it was difficult to swim at all in the crashing waves.

Kip's heart was beating rapidly. What was happening to his safe, snug world?

A powerful wave hit Kip's mother. Kip was torn from her arms. His tiny body

bounced on the waves. He bawled and bawled. But the howling wind was the only sound his mother heard. Her pitiful cries mixed with the roar of the storm.

Many otters, even adults, are injured or killed in storms.

As suddenly as the storm began, it stopped. The female's sad cries went on and on. Where was her baby? She searched for him up and down the beach.

Then she heard a low gurgling sound. It was coming from a pile of rocks just offshore.

She made her way toward the sound. Kip was lying on his side. He was gasping for breath.

His mother took him in her arms. She held him close. She squeezed him. She nuzzled her face against his.

Kip coughed hard. Up came salt water.

Holding her baby under her arm, the female otter swam back to the kelp bed. They were both safe.

CHAPTER 4

Kip was only a few weeks old. He groomed himself. He was not very good at it. But he knew it was important.

Otters must clean themselves a lot. An otter's fur is thicker than any other mammal's. In one square inch, there are over 600,000 hairs. And there are up to a billion over an otter's whole body.

An otter's life depends on his fur. Sea otters do not have a layer of fat, or blubber, under their skins. Other sea mammals do. Blubber provides warmth.

Instead, an otter has two layers of hair. As the otter moves in the water, air bubbles build up between the layers. The bubbles hold in the body heat.

The fur mats if it gets dirty. Then it cannot hold the air bubbles. Cold water can touch the skin. The animal can die.

The more otters groom themselves, the more they fluff up the underfur to trap the air bubbles. Otters even fluff their hair by blowing on it.

Sea otters were hunted heavily for their fur. Those thick, soft furs were very valuable.

The sea otter almost became extinct by the early 1900s. Until then, there had been a lot of otters in the coastal waters of the North Pacific Ocean.

A law was passed in 1911. Sea otters could no longer be hunted. But by then, they were almost extinct.

There were no otters off the coast of Oregon and Washington. And once, large herds had lived there.

In 1938, a few otters were found living along the California coast. More were spotted a few years later. The sea otters returned little by little.

Though they are plentiful once more, they still face dangers. Sea otters are injured or killed by motorboats and jet skis. They are caught in fishermen's gill nets. And many are killed from oil spills.

In 1971, an underground nuclear test explosion was set off. It was on an island near Alaska. About 1,000 sea otters were killed. Other wildlife was killed too.

Sea otters are in the weasel family. Their scientific name is *Enhydra lutris,* which means "otter in the water."

Otters have been sea animals for about a million years. Before then, they lived on land. They lived with dolphins, porpoises, and whales. Seals, sea lions, and walrus. They lived with manatees and **dugongs.** But for some reason, they all left the land and took to the sea.

> **A dugong is a water mammal. It is also called a *sea cow.***

Sea otters are the smallest of all sea mammals. They are about five feet long. These mammals can weigh up to 85 pounds. Females are smaller than males. A sea otter's life span is 12 to 15 years.

Otters' tails are about a foot long. And they have webbed feet. Their hind feet are like flippers.

They are dark brown with lighter coloring on their heads and the back of the necks. As they grow older, the hair on their heads turns lighter. Some old males

are white-headed. Sea otters are the only sea mammals that have eyelashes.

Sea otters are the only animals that use tools except for humans and other primates. Otters use rocks to break open shells. They also use rocks to loosen creatures fastened to rocks in the water.

If an otter has a favorite rock, it may carry it in a pouch under its front leg. It can also hold as many as four sea urchins in each underarm pouch.

River otters are cousins of sea otters. They are much smaller. They weigh about 20 pounds. Their main food is fish. But they also eat snails, water insects, mice, and even birds that nest on the ground.

A sea otter has only one pup at a time. But the river otter has two to four. Unlike the sea otter, river otters are born with their eyes closed. They have no teeth at birth. Their eyes don't open for several weeks. When they are about two months old, their mother teaches them to swim. Sea otters are born knowing how to swim a little.

5

CHAPTER

Kip was two months old. He could dive in shallow water. And he could stay down for about 30 seconds.

Kip spent his time nursing, sleeping, and playing. Sometimes he would slide off his mother's body. He would float beside her on his back. But the female otter never let him get very far away.

One day, Kip was sleeping on his mother's stomach. A large male otter swam close to them. Kip's mother was eating a sea urchin. It was a few moments before she realized the strange male was near.

Sometimes a dominant male from another raft will bother the smaller otters. They don't often injure the young otters, though.

Most sea otters get along well together. But an older one sometimes likes to show who is boss.

The big male reached out to snatch the sea urchin. The female saw him in time. She let out a fierce growl. She flipped over. She grabbed her baby under her arm. She hissed at the old male.

Kip made a scared screech. What was happening? He clung to his mother.

The female swam into the thick kelp.

The old white-headed male paddled
slowly back to his own raft. He had shown
them who was boss.

Days were good for the young pup. He
had all the good, sweet milk he could hold.
He had a mother who loved him. One who

took good care of him. And one who played with him and kept him well groomed.

Several other female otters had given birth. Now more small pups were in the raft.

The days were getting warmer. New sounds could be heard every day. The squawking and screeching came from newly hatched seagulls. The screams of young brown pelicans sounded from the breeding colonies on the rock cliffs.

Sometimes a small flock of pelicans would fly overhead in single file. From heights of about 30 feet, they would plunge down to catch a fish.

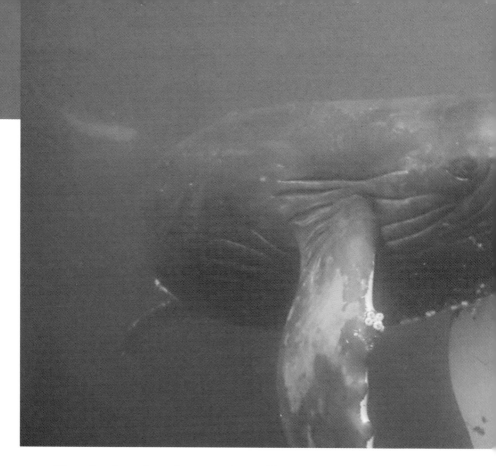

Seals barked nearby. Sometimes they came close to the kelp beds. Young sea otters have been known to play with seals. They would even rub noses with each other.

And once in a while, the song of the humpback whale echoed across the water.

Kip was getting used to the seagulls. They spent a lot of time around the kelp

beds, waiting to feed on the otters' leftovers.

A brave seagull might swoop down and steal a meal from an otter's paw. The first few times this happened, it frightened Kip. Now it made him angry because it upset his mother.

But the stolen food meant nothing to Kip. He still fed only on his mother's milk.

CHAPTER 6

At five months, Kip weighed 12 pounds. He was 23 inches long.

He was eating some solid food. Most of it was caught by his mother. It would be a while before Kip could feed himself entirely.

Kip's mother tore his food into very small pieces. Kip loved the seafood. But he still liked his mother's milk best.

Sometimes Kip's mother did not want to be bothered. So she would turn on her stomach. Then Kip could not get at a nipple.

But if he howled, his mother would usually give in. Sea otter pups are very spoiled.

Kip started diving alone in search of food. He brought up a worthless piece of seaweed. It was the first thing that caught his eye. He often brought up rocks. And once, he found a rusty railroad spike.

However, in time he learned to bring up sea urchins, clams, and other food. By watching his mother, he learned to use a rock as a tool.

Kip could take care of himself by the time he was a year old. He was as big as his mother. When he was fully grown at the age of two or three, he would join a raft of adult males.

Kip learned something important. Thousands of soda and beer cans are thrown into the ocean by thoughtless people.

Small octopuses squeeze into the cans. By watching other otters, Kip learned to tear open the cans with his teeth. Then he would eat the juicy octopuses.

Kip spent more and more time playing with other sea otters his size. And he stole food from the younger pups. Older otters had once done that to him.

Sea otters mainly get along well together. Any spats they have are usually caused by teasing. And otters do love to tease.

Kip had a favorite trick. He would sneak up on an older male who was sleeping. Next he would dive beneath the old otter. Then Kip would bump him with his head and swim away as fast as he could go. Banging rocks together to scare sleeping otters was fun too.

Kip's life would be like one big water party. Although he and the other otters would enjoy eating and sleeping, their favorite pastime would be playing.

CHAPTER 7

Friends of the Sea Otter is a group started in 1968. Its purpose is to protect the sea otter. It was started by Margaret Wentworth Owings and Dr. James Mattison Jr.

Ms. Owings is an artist and a nature lover. She cares deeply about the welfare of the sea otter.

Dr. Mattison is a naturalist. He studies nature and is interested in ocean animals.

Friends of the Sea Otter is based in Monterey, California. The address is

Friends of the Sea Otter
2150 Garden Road, Suite B4
Monterey, CA 93940.

There are over 4,000 members in the group. The money from membership dues and the gift store helps support the program. There are about a dozen board

members in this organization. Among the honorary committee members are Jane Goodall and Robert Redford.

There are about 2,400 sea otters along the coast of Monterey. The group has a sea otter spotting program.

In the gift store, they sell books and videos about sea otters. They sell clothing, jewelry, and plush otters. There are other items dealing with sea otters too.

Volunteers answer questions and explain their programs to visitors. They also provide information to students for research projects. They talk to school groups and organizations.

The group publishes a magazine called *The Otter Pup.* It is the only magazine about sea otters and their habitat.

The group gave a special grant to Russian biologists. It helps them study sea otters. The group also started a program to help animals saved from oil spills.

For over 30 years, the Friends of Sea Otters has fought to keep the sea otter from becoming extinct.